How to Paint Trees In Watercolor

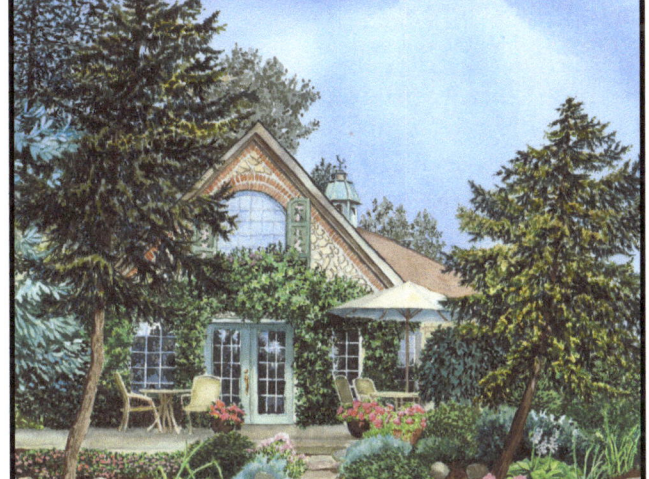

by Debbie Waldorf Johnson

Copyright © 2014 by Debbie Waldorf Johnson

Table of Contents

Review of Basic Painting Skills

Before starting your project, review some of the basic skills required in watercolor painting.

When preparing for a wash (application of paint in a watercolor painting) always begin with a big puddle of wet paint in your palette.

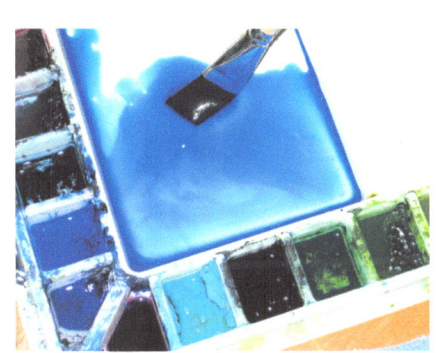

Draw four loose rectangles on a piece of watercolor paper. Each rectangle should be about four by five inches, approximately. Draw these loosely; there is no need to use a ruler! Use these four rectangles to practice the following basic painting skills.

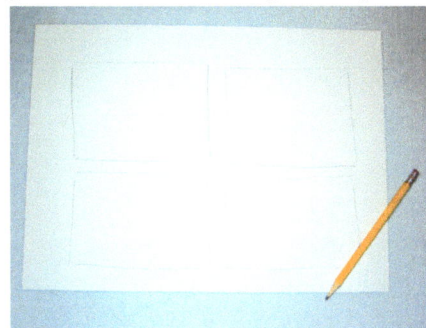

Flat Wash - an even distribution of color in a small or large area. This is the foundational wash for all other washes used in watercolor painting.

Hold your paper in your non-painting hand at a slight angle resting the side of the paper that is closest to your palette on the table and lifting the other edge of the paper about 25-35 degrees above the table. Start at the high end so that your paint will float toward the next stroke. Using a one-inch flat wash brush, draw a wet line of paint across the rectangle from the far edge toward the edge that is

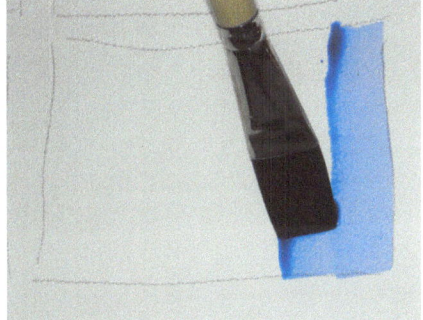

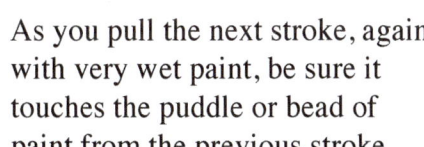

closest to your body.. The paint should be wet enough to leave a bead or puddle of wet paint along the edge of your mark.

As you pull the next stroke, again with very wet paint, be sure it touches the puddle or bead of paint from the previous stroke. This pulls the wetness into the next stroke. Continue holding the paper at a slight angle to keep the bead at the bottom edge of the stroke so that you can touch it again when making the next stroke.

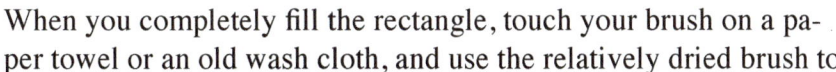

When you completely fill the rectangle, touch your brush on a paper towel or an old wash cloth, and use the relatively dried brush to

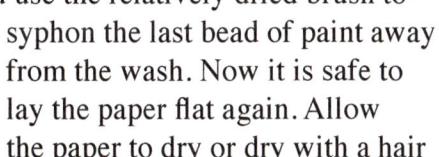

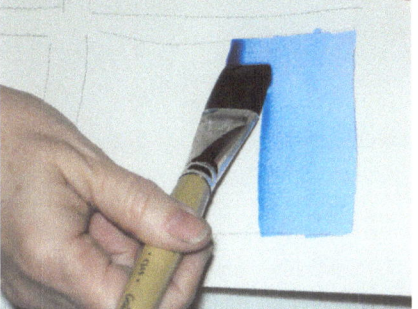

syphon the last bead of paint away from the wash. Now it is safe to lay the paper flat again. Allow the paper to dry or dry with a hair dryer. If using a hair dryer hold it at a distance so that the air does not move the pigment particles that are floating in the wet paint.

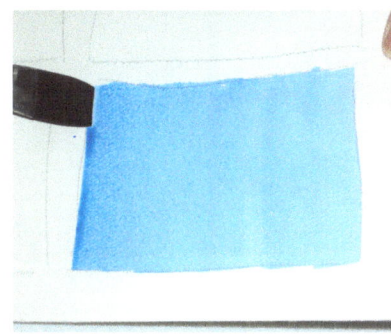

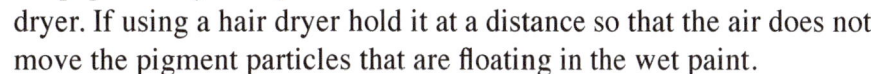

The goal of a flat wash is to create a flat, smooth area of even color.

View a video of this technique at:
http://www.youtube.com/watercolorworks

3

Graded Wash – a wash that starts with a darker value and progresses to a lighter value.
The same principle that is used for a flat wash is also used in creating a graded wash. The difference is that as each stroke is applied, a small amount of water is added to the brush to make the pigment more diluted. This creates a nice value change, which can be used in almost every painting. It is especially great for skies.

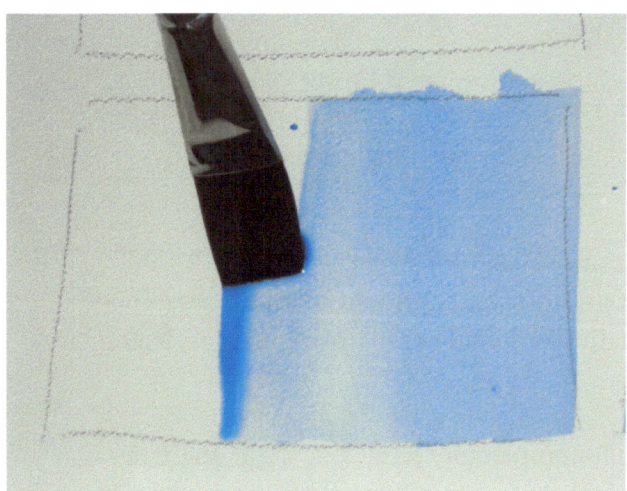 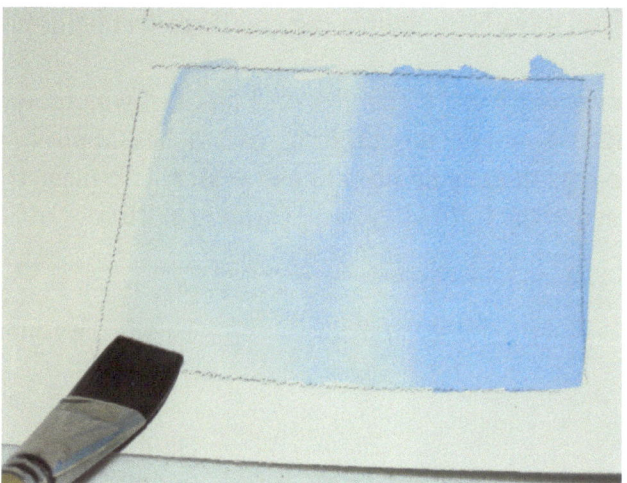

Blended Wash – a wash that contains two or more colors that meet at wet edges to blend together and appear soft.

Again use the same technique to lay down color as you would a flat wash. This time, clean your brush and change pigment part way through. Notice that as the second color touches the bead of the first color, it creates a soft edge. If both colors are very wet and the paper is tipped back and forth, they will physically mix to create a soft blend of new color.

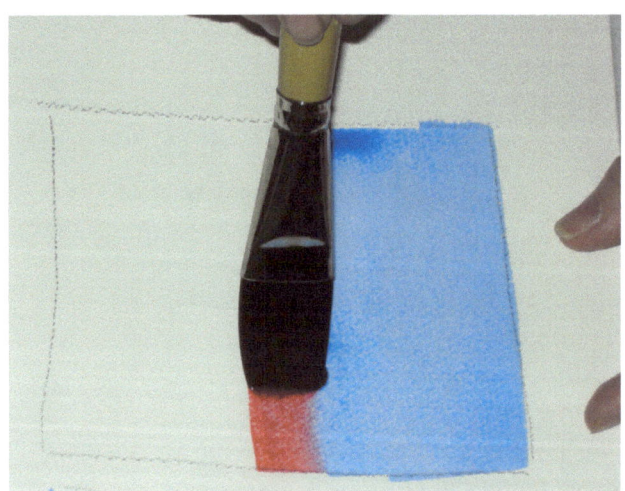 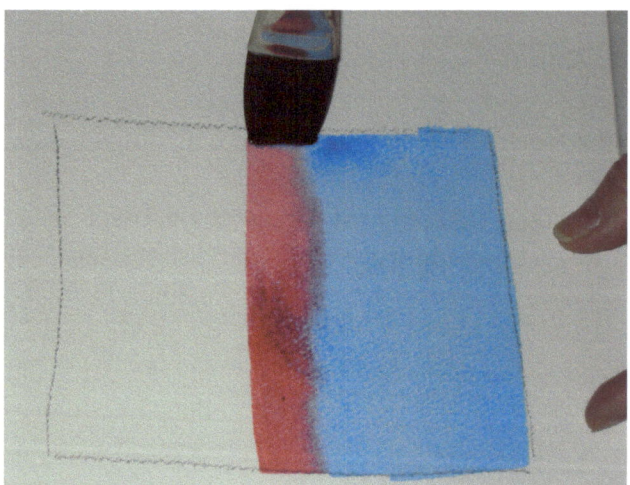

View a video of this technique at:
http://www.youtube.com/watercolorworks

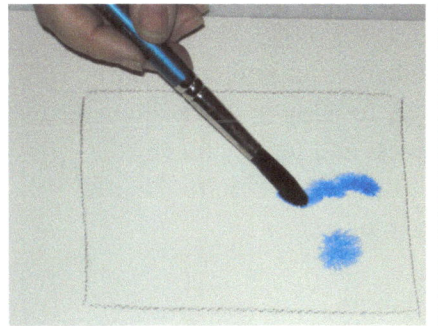 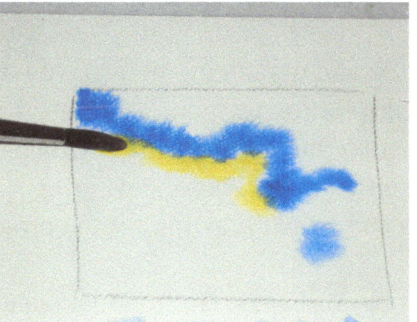 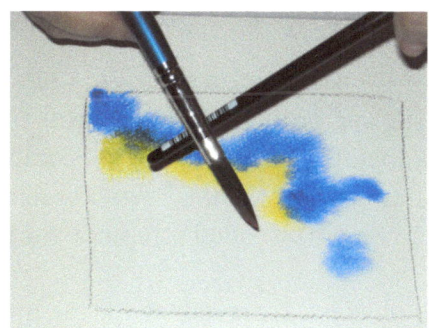

Wet-in-Wet Wash – a varied wash of several colors applied on a wet surface.

Wet-in-wet washes are fun, yet difficult to control. Wet one of your rectangles with plain water or a light color. Completely cover the rectangle. Allow the water to absorb into the paper so there are no standing puddles, but you do want a glossy appearance to the area.

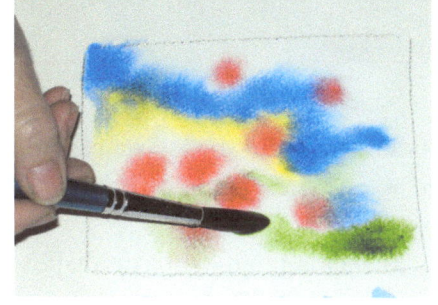

Next, drip or paint strong pigments into the wet areas. Use several colors and experiment. You can also tap a loaded brush onto the handle of another brush to splash pigment into the wet area. Tipping the paper will blend the colors more; leaving the paper flat will help to control the blending.

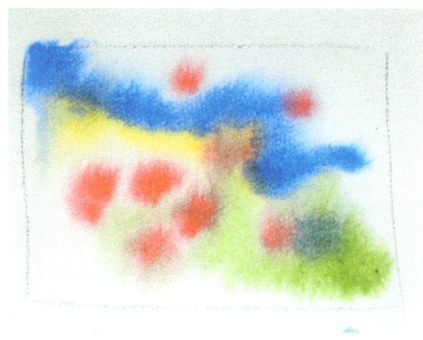

Calligraphic Linework – line work of pigment developed using all edges of a brush at various angles. Practice using all of your brushes and see how many marks you can make with each. Hold the brush straight up and down, hold it at a drastic angle, and push and lift it as you pull pigment across the paper. Try to write your name in cursive with each brush you have. Explore what your brushes can do for you!

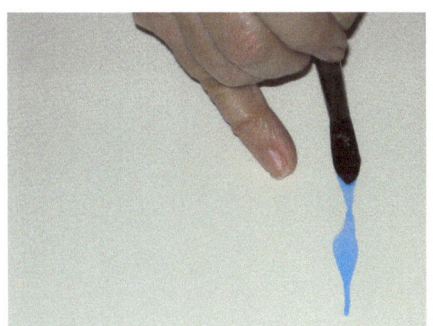 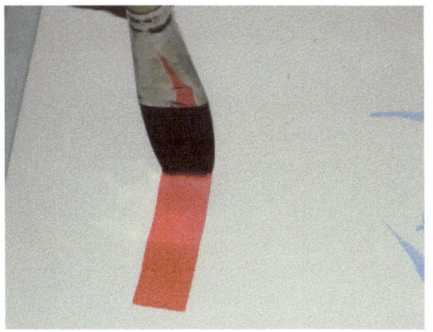 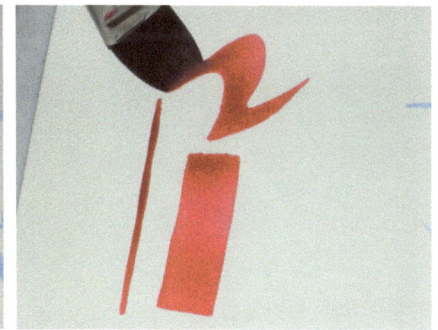

Dry Brush/Scumble – line work of pigment developed using relatively dry paint and a variety of brush strokes. Use less pigment in an almost-dry brush to create sketchy, expressive strokes with a variety of brushes. This is a great technique to develop textures in wood or natural objects.

View a video of this technique at:
http://www.youtube.com/watercolorworks

Using Photo References

Always use your own photos. Collecting and organizing photos from magazines and other sources is fun and provides rich resources for inspiration for your paintings. I enjoy looking at professional photographs as inspiration for composition, but I always use my own objects and photos for my paintings. Once you take photos that suit your desires for a painting it is time to move on to the next step. I have provided reference photos and a final drawing for the project in this book.

All objects can be reduced to the most basic shapes: circle, square, and triangle.

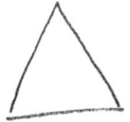  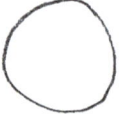 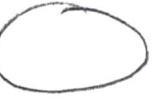

From those basic shapes we can add shading and distortion to make cones, rectangles, cylinders, ovals, and so on. These simple shapes are found everywhere in nature.

Try to sketch the most basic shapes (triangles, cones, squares, ovals) from the photos on this page.

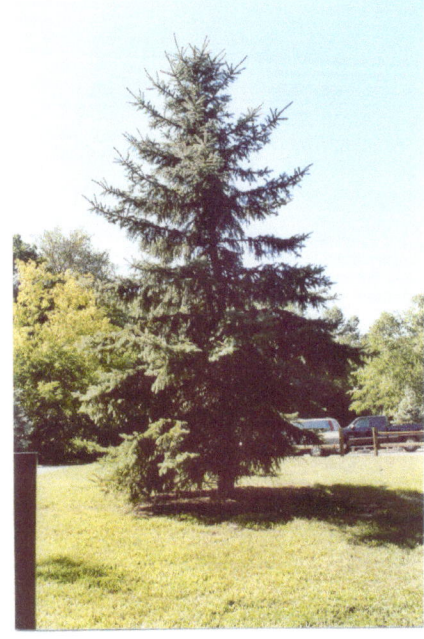

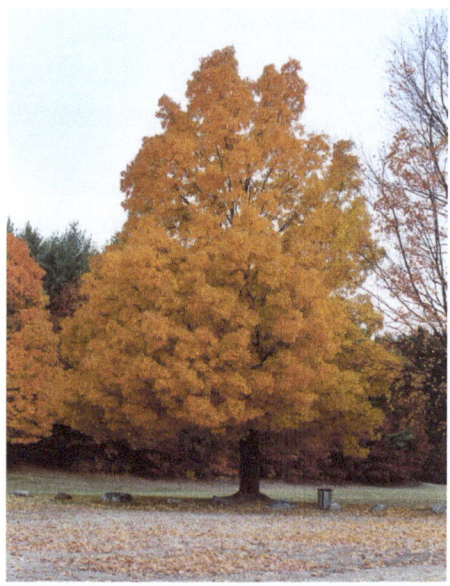

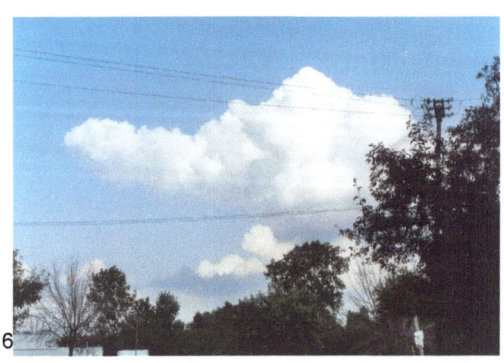

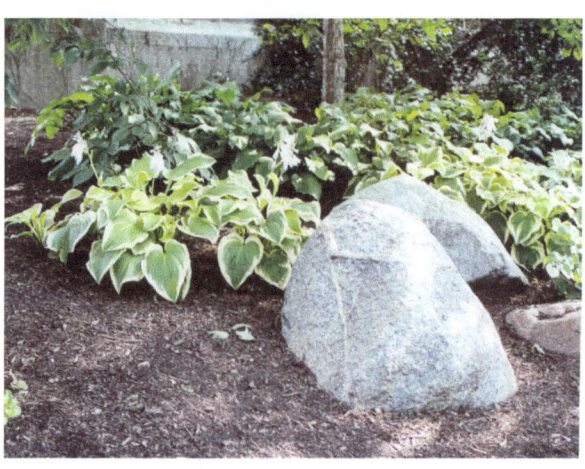

Planning Your Composition

Even though you did a lot of work on your composition at the setup stage, there is still a little more work to do. The more thoroughly you work out the details before-hand the more fun your painting process will be. Whatever problems you neglect to work out at this stage will haunt you throughout the painting.

Try to sketch the most basic shapes (triangles, cones, squares, ovals, etc.) from your composition in your sketchbook. Place the objects in a pleasing way on your paper. Don't worry about any details until the basic shapes are in the correct places.

Now you will develop some thumbnail sketches from your basic shapes. Thumb-nail sketches should be small and should be used for problem solving before you ever touch your watercolor paper. They are quick, sketchy little drawings of the basic shapes you are looking at. Thumbnails help you to quickly move objects around your picture plane, work on value contrast and de-velop a basic composition for your painting.

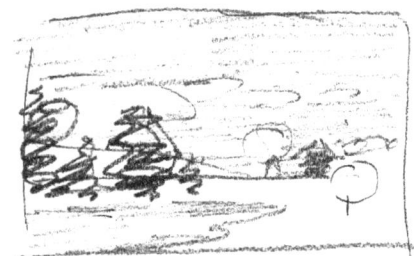

Remember to minimize the shapes to help you work quickly. This is not a final drawing, just a method to work out the most important aspects of your painting: composition and value. If your composition and values are right, your painting will be a success.

Things to think about while developing thumbnail sketches:
• Do I want to make this painting in a horizontal or vertical format?
• Do I want all of the objects to appear in whole or do I want to cut some off at the edges?
• How can I add more interest?
• Is this painting flat or are there interesting changes in plane, line and position?
• Where is my horizon line?
• What are the basic shapes of the objects I want to add to my painting?
• How do the sizes of the shapes relate to one another?
• Are the distant objects smaller than the closer objects?
• How dark or light are the objects compared to each other?
• Where do I want the focal point or point of interest in my painting to be?
• How can I draw the viewers interest to the focal point? Use details, color, value contrast?
• Is this a subject that will keep me interested the entire timeI work on it?
• What details can I leave out of this piece?
• What details are essential to the piece?
• Is this painting telling a story, expressing an idea, telling something about the artist, or simply being painted for the pleasure of painting?
• Is there a dominant color in the painting?
• Are the colors leaning toward cool or warm?
• Is there a strong sense of light and dark to define the volume of the shapes?

Thumbnail Sketches

1. Look for the basic shapes in your composition.
   - Is it a triangle shape, a round shape, a rectangular shape?
   - Is it bigger on top than on the bottom?
   - Is it pear-shaped?
   - Is it soft-edged, crisp, or angular?
   - Are some objects overlapping?
   - Are there spaces between objects?
   - Can you see the trunk or is it within the bulk of the foliage?
   - What shapes are the "empty" areas?
   - Where does the focal area fall in the picture plane?
     (Hint: draw a grid to help locate specific elements and get their relationship to one another correct.)

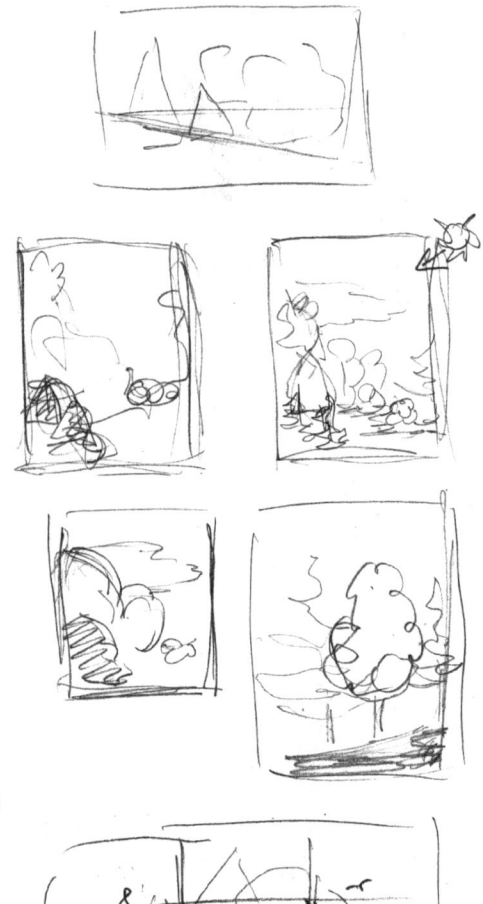

2. After capturing the basic outer shape of the objects, and their placement on the picture plane, ask yourself the same questions from step 1 about the individual parts: shadow shapes, individual branches, limbs, clumps of foliage, and so on. Also ask yourself:
   - Do the branches reach up or swing out and down?
   - Is there a lot of foliage or just a little?
   - Is the foliage evenly dispersed or heavier in one area?
   - Are branches close together or is there space between them?
   - Is there a crisp edge to the shadow shape or does it gently grade from dark to light?
   - Are the shapes correctly sized compared to each other?

3. Now think in values.
   - Use your value scale* and think light = value 1; dark = value 6.
   - Mark the numbers 1 – 6 on your thumbnail to relate to the values.
   - If you have combined photo references for a better composition, decide the values for the added elements.
   - Pay attention to areas in shadow and in light.
   - Shade in the values according to your numbers with a pencil.

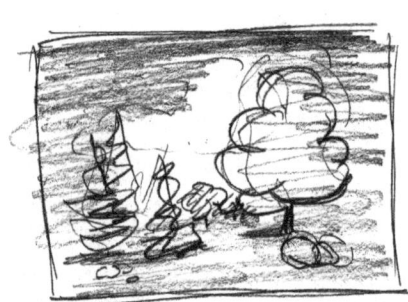

*A value scale is available in the reference photos section in this book.

Thumbnail sketches are not final drawings. They are simply a method to work out solutions to common composition and value problems. Focus not on drawing but on the most basic elements of the picture.

Preparing a Drawing

There are lots of ways to develop drawings for your paintings. Once you have developed a thumbnail sketch that you think fits your goals for the painting you can then make a larger drawing to match the size of your desired finished painting. Transfer this drawing to your watercolor paper.

Many of my students don't enjoy the drawing process as much as painting or simply don't have strong drawing skills, so I help them find simpler, easier ways to develop their drawings. Many fine, professional watercolor artists use slides or computers to help them in this process. Others use a grid system, which works very well. Others simply rely on the basics in their thumbnail sketches to get the simple ideas down, and then paint in a looser fashion, not worrying about the details at all.

If you have strong drawing skills, producing the drawing by hand from your references and thumbnails is the best approach. If you are anxious to paint or don't have strong drawing skills, you can make a small drawing by tracing your photos over a light box or by holding them up to a brightly lit window. Then, when you have the basic shapes and some of the details you want to capture in your drawing you can use a photocopier to enlarge the components and place them on the proper size drawing paper for your desired painting.

No matter how you prepare your drawing, make sure you develop it through sketching and study; this is crucial to a successful painting. This is the stage where you work out the road map for your painting. Take the time to sketch and get intimately familiar with the shapes and values of all the objects you want in your painting. You may even want to develop small watercolor sketches of the piece to work out color problems that may arise.

Now that you have a developed drawing, let's transfer it to your prepared watercolor paper. Remember, the drawing should be the exact size of the desired finished painting, or the same size as your watercolor sheet.

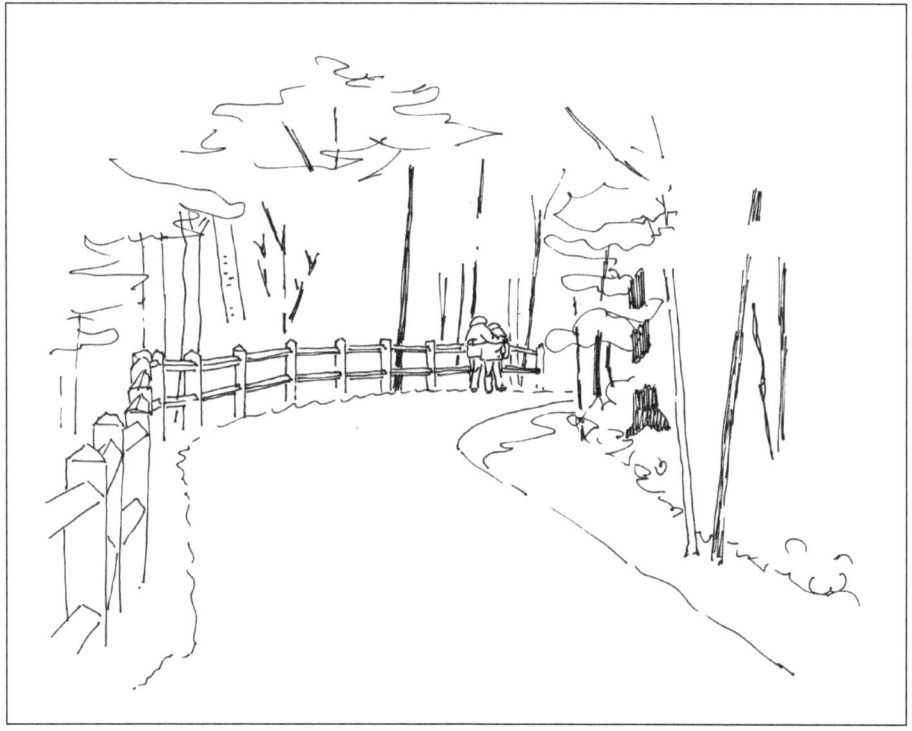

How to Prepare Watercolor Paper

What you will need:
- Foam core board at least three inches bigger than your watercolor paper on all sides.
- Clear packing tape
- Two-inch wide masking tape
- Scissors
- Watercolor paper

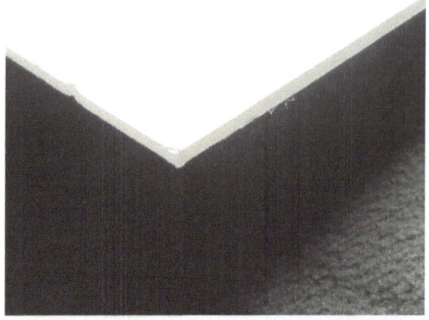

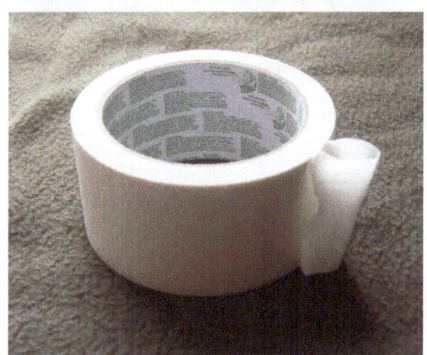

Some artists stretch wet paper onto heavy boards to keep the sheets flat while painting. I prefer the simple method of mounting dry paper onto foam core board to maintain the integrity of my paper while painting.

The process that I use protects the areas of the foam core board where you will eventually tape your watercolor paper. The clear packing tape prevents the masking tape from tearing the foam core and it slightly waterproofs the edges to protect it when applying juicy washes onto your painting. This board, if properly prepared, will be useful for many paintings in the future. It is a lightweight alternative to traditional watercolor paper stretching.

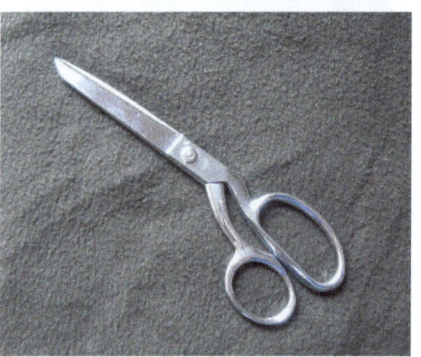

1. Cut the foam core board so that it measures about two inches larger than your watercolor paper on all sides.

2. Tape the outer edges of the foam core with clear packing tape. Cover the edges with at least two rows of tape on all sides, front and back. This board may be used over and over again as a support for your watercolor paper.

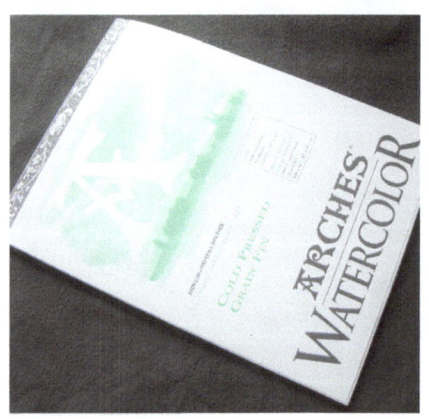

Tape watercolor paper to prepared foam core board with masking tape. Be sure that at least one half inch of your watercolor paper is covered with the tape to secure it to the board. Remember, your paper will get wet while painting. This will cause it to buckle, warp and stretch. The secure application of tape will hold it firmly to the foam core during the painting process.

Your framer will appreciate the fact that your artwork was stretched to stay flat. Framing a warped or bowed watercolor is very difficult.

Now you are ready to transfer a drawing to your paper.

Transfer the Drawing to Watercolor Paper

What you will need:
- Watercolor paper
- Completed drawing and thumbnail sketches
- Photo references
- Chunky graphite stick
- Pencil for tracing
- Prepared foam core stabilizer board
- Two-inch-wide masking tape

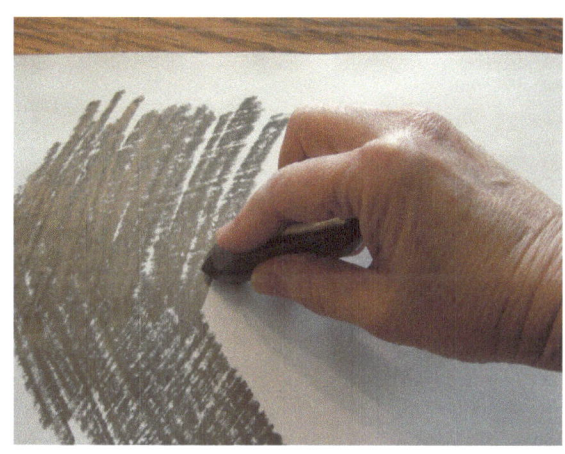

1. Scrub the chunky graphite stick on the back of your completed drawing. Use a little elbow grease to get good coverage over the entire image area.

2. Use a tissue to gently smooth over the graphite to release loose crumbs and to fill in the spaces where the graphite didn't completely cover the paper. Use a light touch.

3. Wash your hands! This will keep your watercolor paper clean.

4. Use a strip of masking tape and secure the drawing on one edge to your watercolor paper, like a hinge. This will allow you to lift the drawing occasionally to check your progress, without losing your alignment.

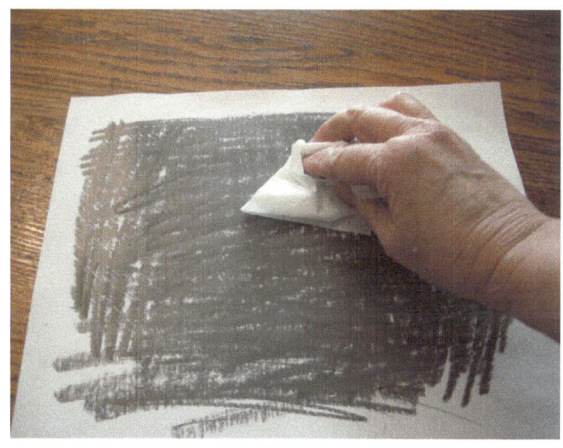

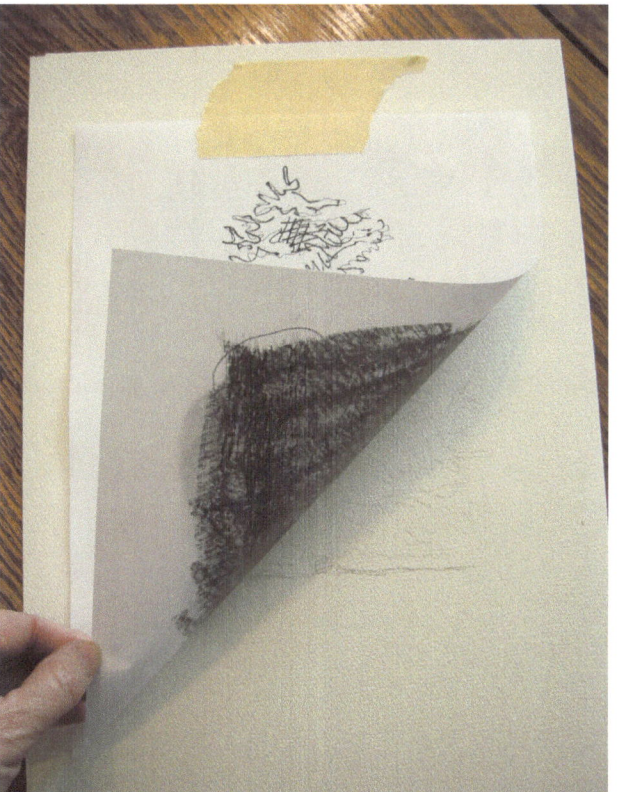

5. Trace your image using a pencil or an ink pen. Be gentle so that you do not dent the watercolor paper. You only need to press hard enough to deposit the graphite image lightly onto the paper.

6. Carefully lift off the drawing paper and fold it in half so that the graphite is on the inside of the fold.

7. Now you can use a pencil to correct any markings you may want to fix. Using a white vinyl eraser you may also gently erase places where you don't want the graphite.

8. Place your watercolor paper on the prepared foam core board. Secure it with the masking tape. Be sure to cover at least one half inch of the paper edges with the tape to keep it from buckling when wet. Now you are ready to paint!

An alternative method is to use graphite transfer paper purchased from an art supply store.

Sample Photo References

Here are sample reference photos from which you can work.

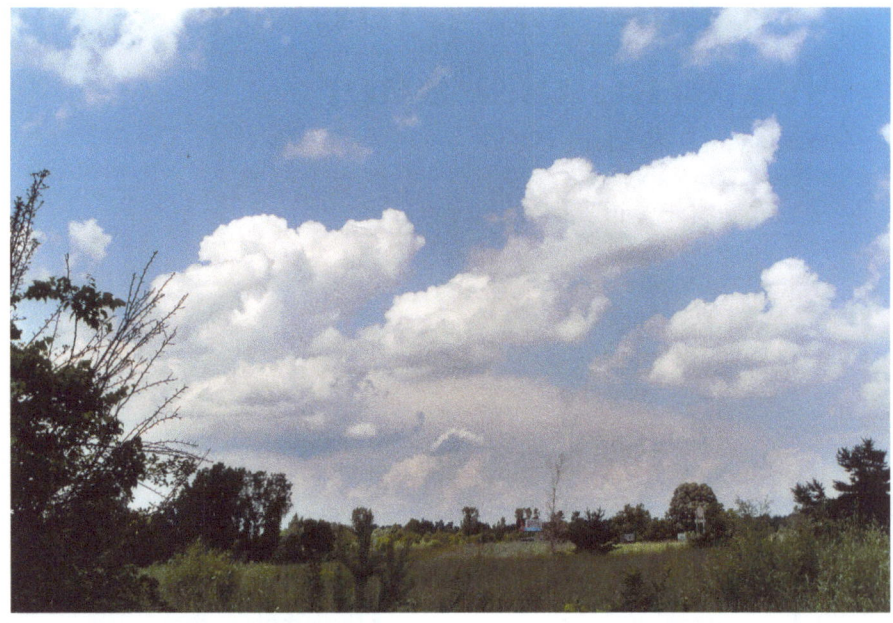

Sky

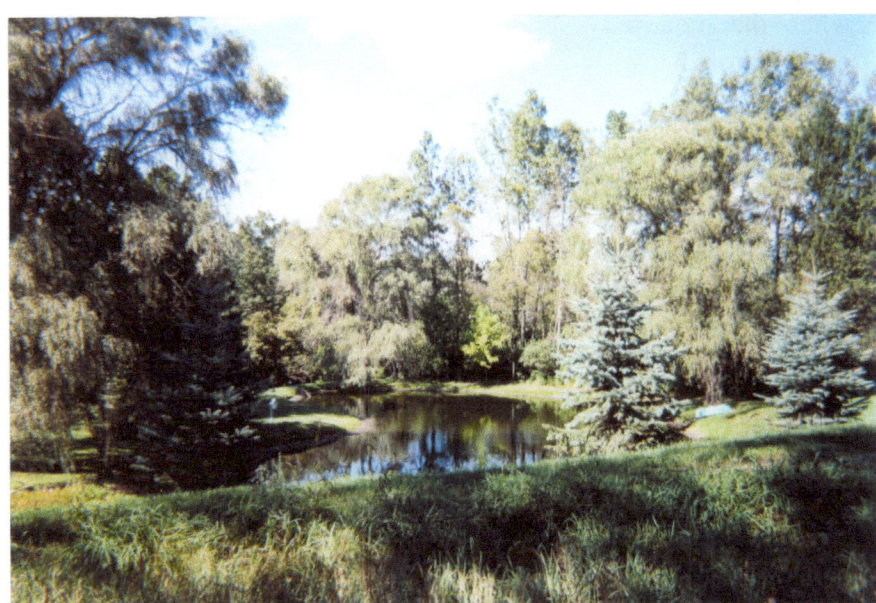

Experiment with *thumbnail sketches using these references. Mix elements from each photo to create your own unique composition.*

Pond/Water and trees

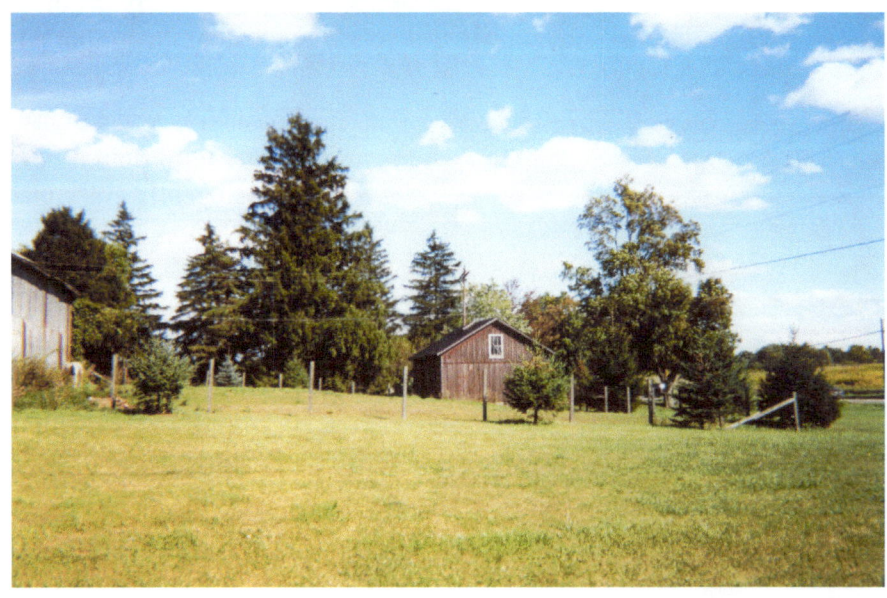

Foundation reference — trees, horizon line and building.

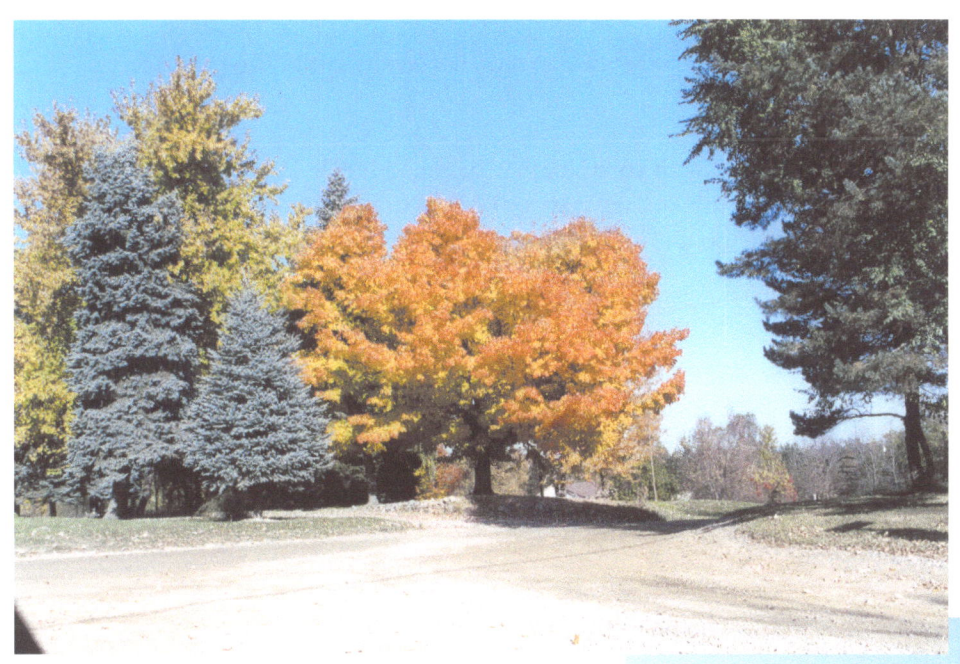

Autumn Scene

Palm Trees

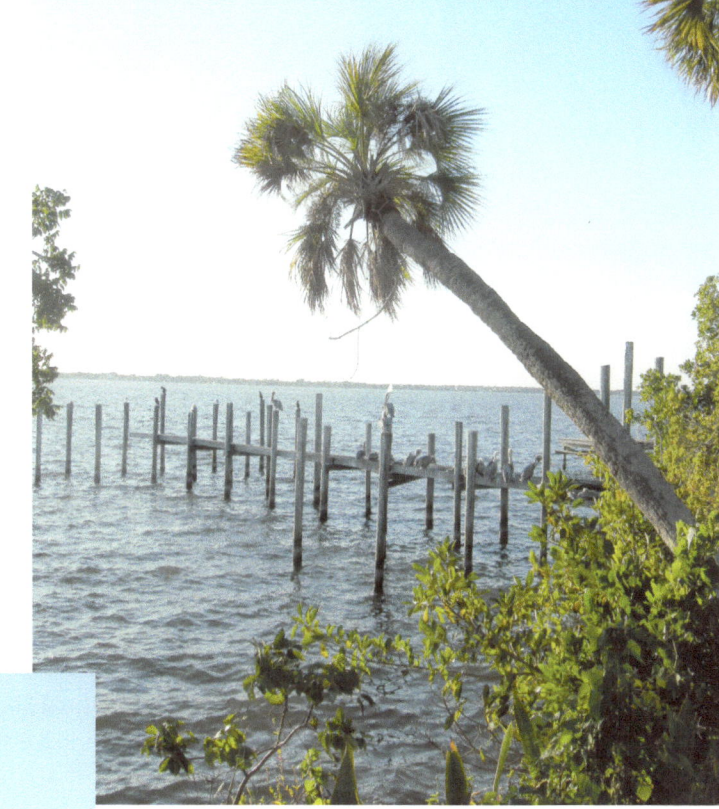

Practice with Branches

Practice with Branches:

1. Begin with light colors. Use a dance-like motion with your Number 10 round brush. Focus on moving the handle in different directions to get a variety of brush strokes that convey the impression of leaves. Go slowly and think about making the marks varied. If they are too uniform your painting will look contrived and not natural.

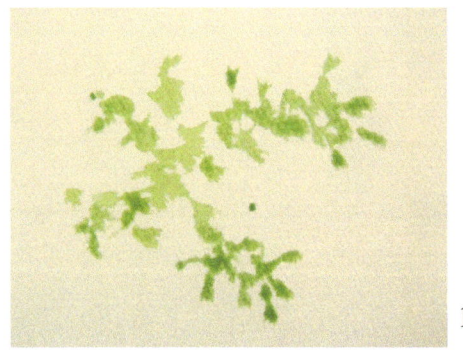

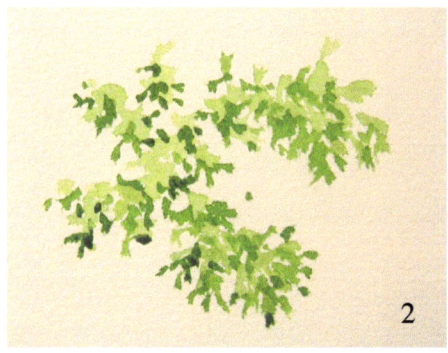

2. Progress with different colors, drying thoroughly between applications. Pay attention to the shapes that form the clumps of leaves. Also pay attention to the light side and the shadow side of the clumps.

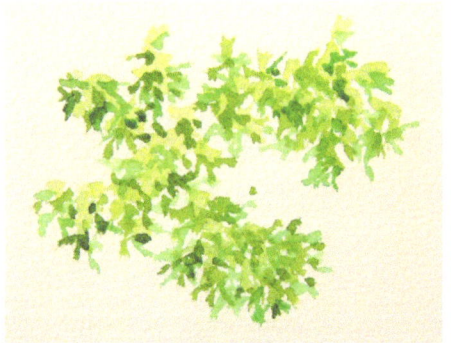

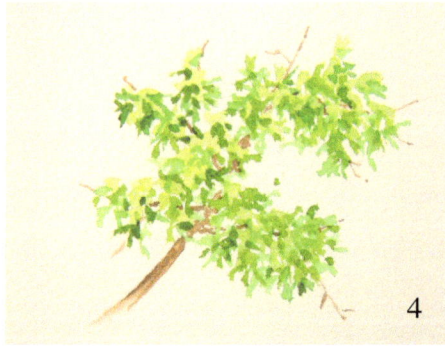

3. Now you can begin to use your Number 6 round brush. Don't let yourself get too tight with the detail. Continue to allow your brush to bounce and dance around the branches.

4. Add branches and twigs to create a realistic foundation for your branch.

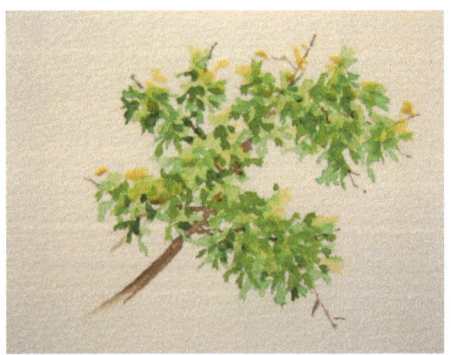

5. In the final stage, I added a glaze of yellow in just a few areas to add some sparkle.

Practice with Deciduous Trees

1. Begin with light colors. Use a dance-like motion with your Number 10 round brush. Focus on moving the handle in different directions to get a variety of brush strokes to convey the impression of leaves. This is where familiarity and comfort with your brushes comes in handy. I call this motion a "brush dance" because it looks like my brush is dancing over the paper. Be sure to allow each color application to dry thoroughly before applying the next. A hair dryer works well.

1

2. Look at the overall shape of the leaf clumps. They are like ovals in this type of tree. Each oval will have a light side and a shadow side, similar to a ball or an egg. Build each oval clump of leaves with light and shadow, painting with one value at a time.

2

3. As you build each glaze of color, each layer should get a little darker. Dry between layers. Now you can expand the shape of the ovals with leaves that stick out from the bottom and sides. Remember to allow some of your lightest colors to shine through the darker areas. Don't completely fill in the areas. This creates a sparkle and life to the tree, just as it looks in nature when the light shines on the moving leaves.

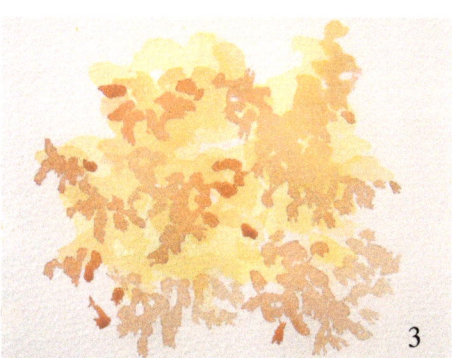

3

4. Add trunk and branches sparingly. Too much of this and it will look overworked.

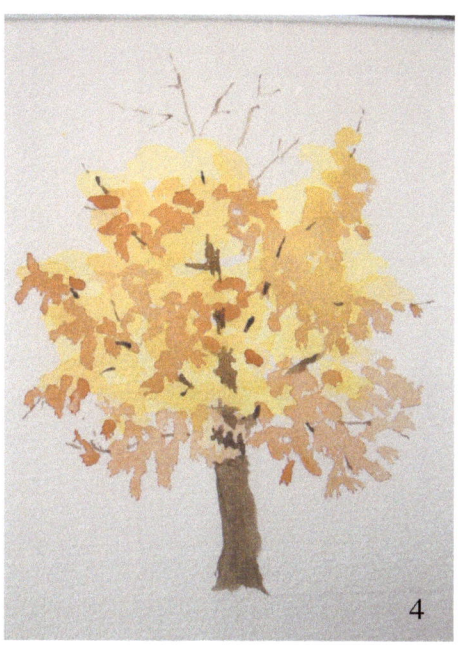

4

Practice with Evergreen Trees

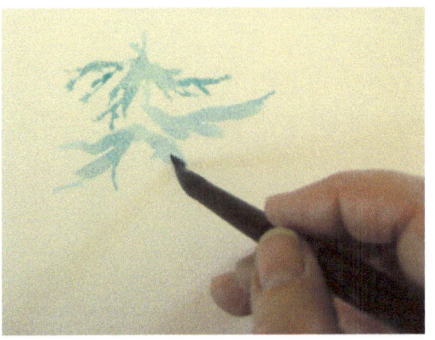

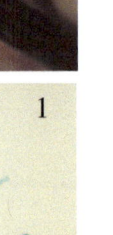

1. Developing an evergreen tree is similar to the other trees, except you will use more of a gliding motion and the tip of your brush. Pull the paint out and down with each stroke to mimic the direction of the branches of each pine bow.

Start with light colors and broader strokes and work to darker values with thinner, more controlled strokes. Just as with the other trees, allow each glaze of color to dry thoroughly before applying the next.

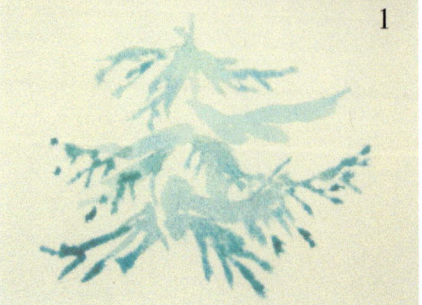

2. The shadow characteristics of the pine tree will have a more elongated, hanging look. Be sure to leave lots of room between the pine bows to keep the tree from looking like a big triangle. This is called the negative space — the space between branches.

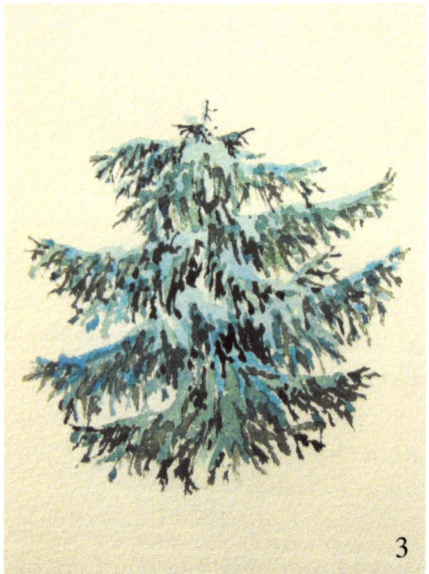

3. As you build the shadows of the branches keep your brush in an upright position in order to make better use of the tip of the brush. I call this brush stroke the pull-push stroke. Vary the colors of the brushwork to add life and vitality to the tree. Shadow areas can contain darker blues and even browns to add to this variety in color.

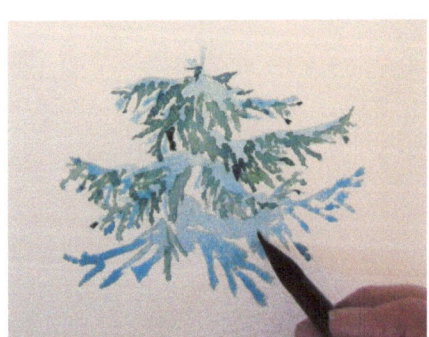

4. Add the trunk and branches. Remember to keep this part simple. Note that most evergreen trees have one main upright trunk. The branches are usually quite well hidden under the green needles.

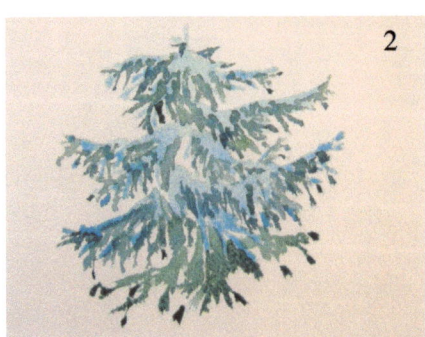

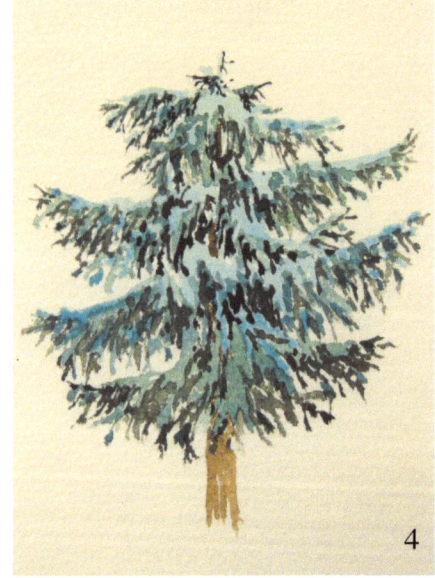

View a video of this technique at:
http://www.youtube.com/watercolorworks

16

Practice with Palm Trees

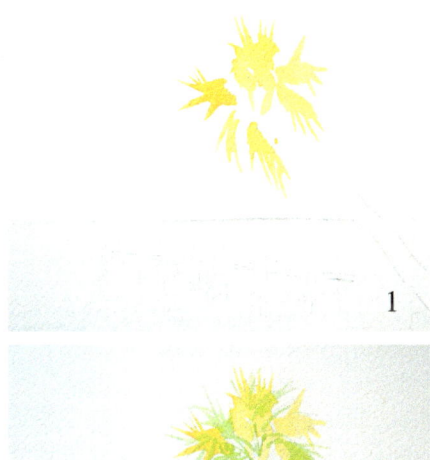

1. The development of a palm tree is similar to the other trees in the progression of colors. The stroke is what I call a pull-push stroke. Hold the brush nearly straight up and down so only the tip touches the paper. To get a nice, clean stroke first take breath, then as you gently let the breath out through your mouth, glide the brush, ever so lightly, onto the paper. This breath action will calm your hand and give your more control. You will pull the brush toward you and lift gently at the end of the stroke. This will give the illusion of a long, thin leaf that is thicker at one end and thinner at the other end.

Start with light colors and work to darker colors just as with the other trees, allowing each glaze of color to dry thoroughly before applying the next.

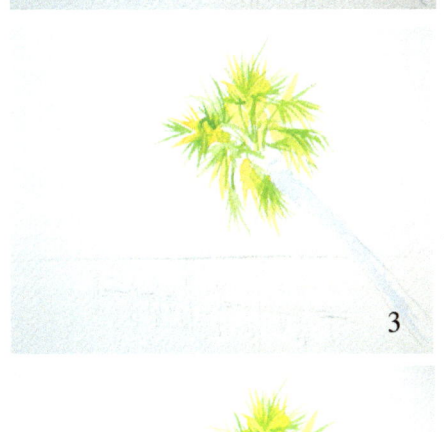

2. Look for where the light is coming from in your reference photo. The shadows, and darker colors, will be on the opposite side of the clump of leaves. Keep this direction of light consistent for a look of realism. Vary the direction of the strokes, always using your photo reference for clues as to direction and volume.

3. Add a stroke of blue to the trunk to keep the browns from being too warm and to enhance the shadow areas. This particular trunk has a gray quality and the blue under-painting will keep it on the gray side.

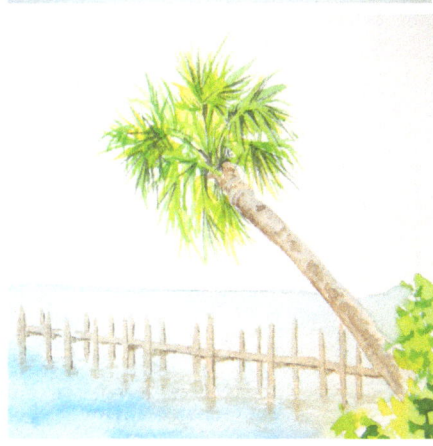

4. Continue to add glazes of darker greens to the top of the palm tree and add details to the trunk and other areas of the painting. It is best to work from light to dark. Don't over work. Be sure to stop before you think you should to avoid a fussy-looking painting.

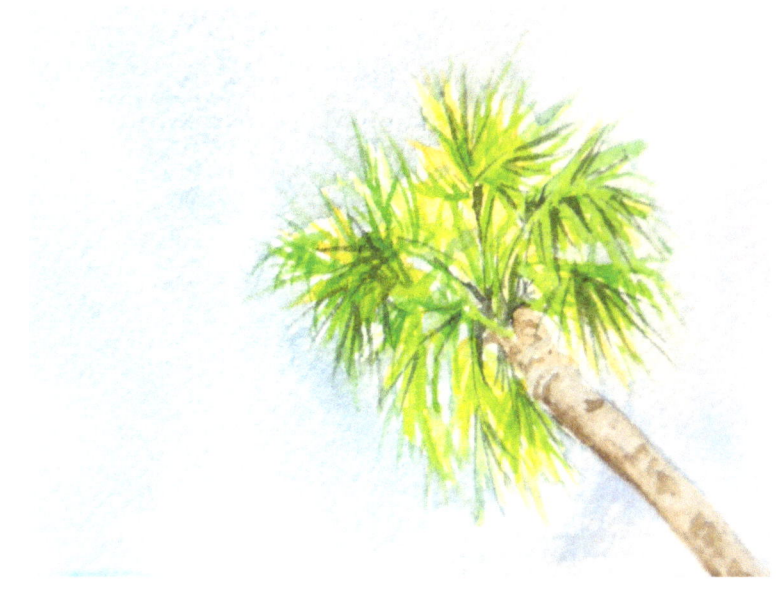

4

Now Let's Paint!!!

Keep your reference materials close by: photos, thumbnail sketches and any other sketches. Be sure the pigments in your palette are wet and ready to go. Be sure that your work area is set up so that you can work most efficiently. If you are right-handed your palette, water, paper toweling and brushes should be on your right side. If you are left-handed, put all of your materials on your left side. Your paper should be directly in front of you. The photo and drawing reference for the image used in this example are found in the back of this book.

Simplify as you start the painting. Fisrt, look for the largest flat or graded wash areas where you can apply color. You may want to apply the washes under any areas that will appear to be in the back of your foreground objects. This is especially true of areas where the foreground objects are darker in value or will not be affected by the colors applied underneath as the first wash. Watercolor is transparent so if you need a light value or a very different color in one area, do not paint under it with another color. Dry thoroughly after each glaze of color.

Application of paint should follow in order of simplicity, value and size of wash:

SKY - Cloudless or with clouds. Notice that even a cloudless sky has value and color variations. Skies are typcially created with flat or graded washes.

TREES - Begin with the foundation washes of the trees; work on details later. Look for the lightest colors in value. Work wet. Don't worry about line work or details until the very last stage of your painting.

Apply the largest washes first. For the sky, I often wet the area first, then apply the wash. This creates a smooth area of color. I paint the outside areas first, then work the color between the branches.

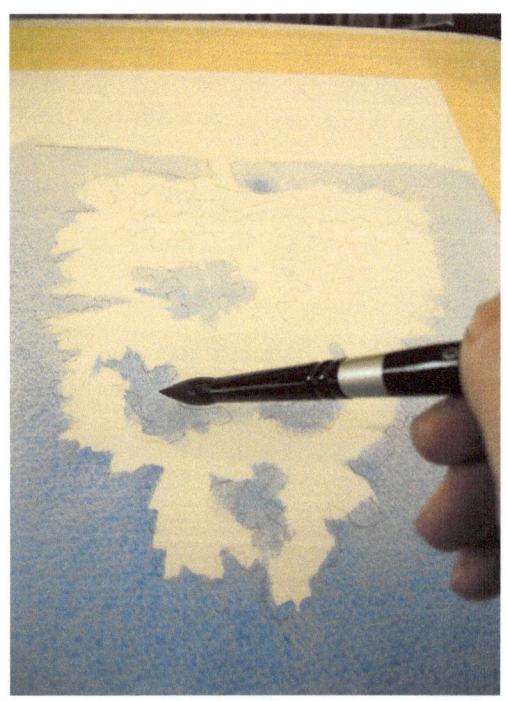

I work the board in all directions, including upside down, in order to maximize my comfort in reaching different areas.

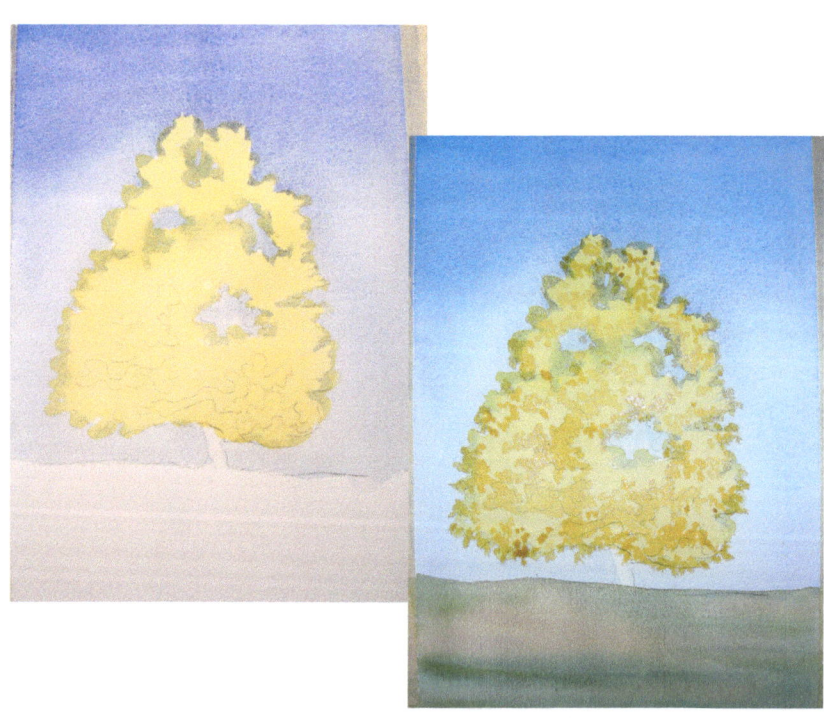

18

Adding Other Elements to Your Landscape

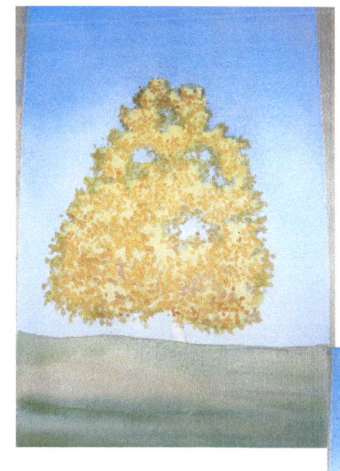

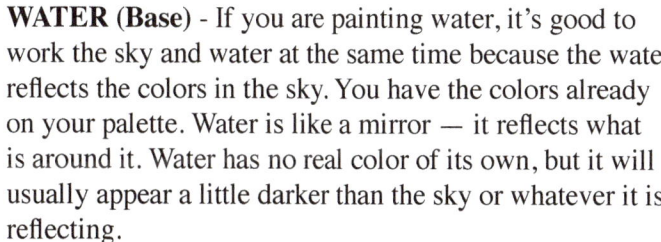

WATER (Base) - If you are painting water, it's good to work the sky and water at the same time because the water reflects the colors in the sky. You have the colors already on your palette. Water is like a mirror — it reflects what is around it. Water has no real color of its own, but it will usually appear a little darker than the sky or whatever it is reflecting.

REFLECTIONS IN WATER - Use the colors that you are using in the trees. Remember even if the water is still the reflections will have some distortion. It will also most likely be darker in the water than the land-based scene.

GRASS - Look at where the sun may be shining and apply warm yellows, golds and greens to these areas. Look for where the shadows are, and apply blues and cool greens to these areas. Work wet and allow the edges to touch and soften. Look for large areas of color and shadow shapes. Do not try to paint every blade of grass.

BACKGROUND TREES AND FIELDS - Look at the value of the colors and shapes of objects in the distance or far from you focal area compared to the objects in and close to the focal area of your painting. If you have to match either color or value, choose value. Also notice that the details of the distant objects are not as apparent. The shapes can be very simple and still read as trees and fields.

STEP BACK AND LOOK FROM A DISTANCE TO KEEP YOURSELF ON TRACK.
Don't fuss over the painting. Enjoy the process.

GETTING BEYOND THE FIRST WASHES - Again pay attention to values. Where is the sun shining and where is the shadow? Shadows will be cooler colors (blue, green, cool browns); areas in sunlight will be warmer colors (yellow, gold, warm reds and browns).

DETAILS, DETAILS, DETAILS - Only put in the details that are *required* to make the piece say what you want it to say or to enhance the composition. If something is not essential to the theme or message of the piece, don't add it. When you think you are *almost* finished...stop. If you go beyond this point you will be in danger of overworking your painting.

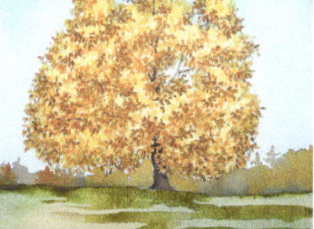

Sample Paintings

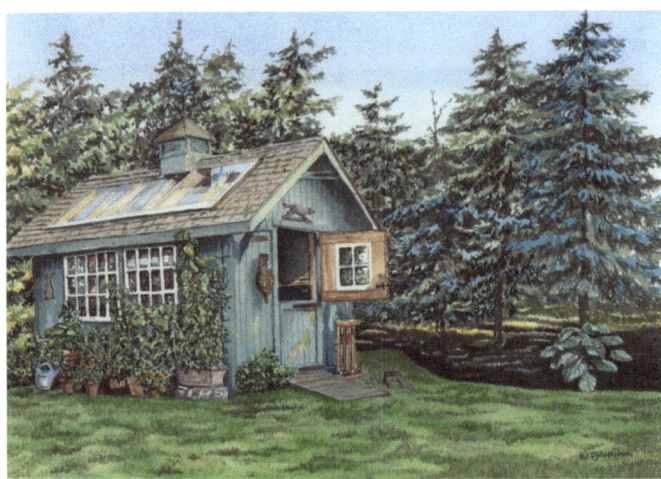

Amish Shed

Here are a few of my finished paintings that use the techniques described in this workbook.

In 'Amish Shed' I used the pull-push stroke to create the line of pine trees behind the garden shed.

I started the painting with a pencil drawing on the watercolor paper. I applied the sky colors, notice the variation in color from darker blue at the very top to lighter blue as the sky moves toward the horizon line. After the sky was dry I applied the lightest flat and graded washes in the larger areas. As the piece progressed I painted more of the details, referring often to the details of my reference photos and sketches. Notice the light and shadow areas near the horizon line under the trees.

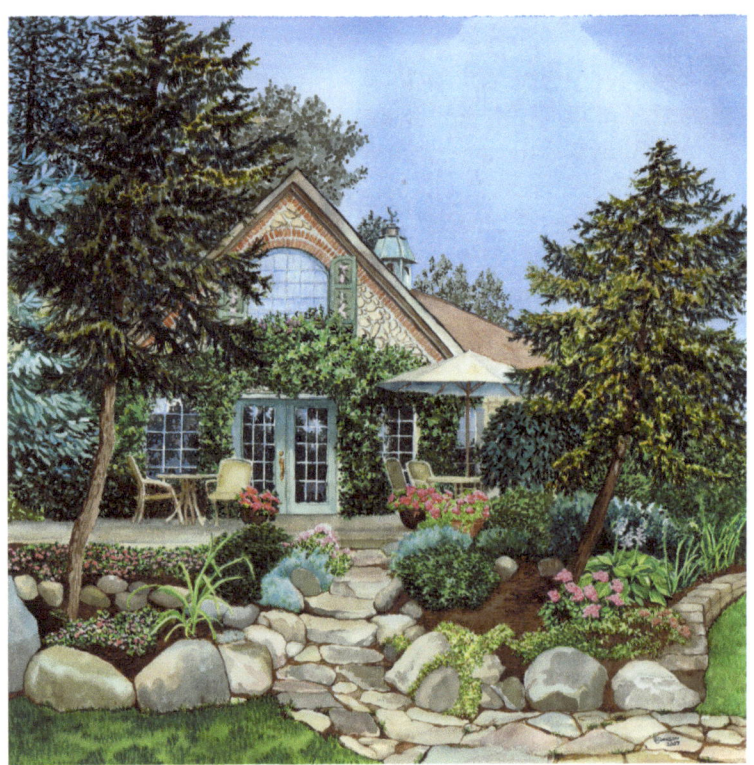

Lockelin Cottage #2

The trees that surround this cottage were very expressive, bent from the wind off the nearby lake. The trees in the background were painted with lighter, more dull variations of the colors used in the foreground trees. This helps the viewer to see they are in the background and they don't compete with the foreground trees.

I tried to use a variety of greens, yellows, and browns to develop the different types of trees in this painting. A white pine and a blue spruce have very different colored needles even though they are both pine trees. They will appear more realistic when painted with colors that are true to their natural hues. Practice glazing different colors from your palette to see the myriad of colors and shades you can produce.

The same techniques used to paint trees can be used to paint plants and buildings. The brush dance stroke was used on the plants and flowers, starting with yellow, then green, then dark green and blue for the shadows.

The texture in the stonework of the building was created using the same brush strokes that I use to paint trees. The dark shadows under the arches of the building were developed with several glazes of French Ultramarine blue and a variety of browns. Each pigment was glazed over dried pigment layers.

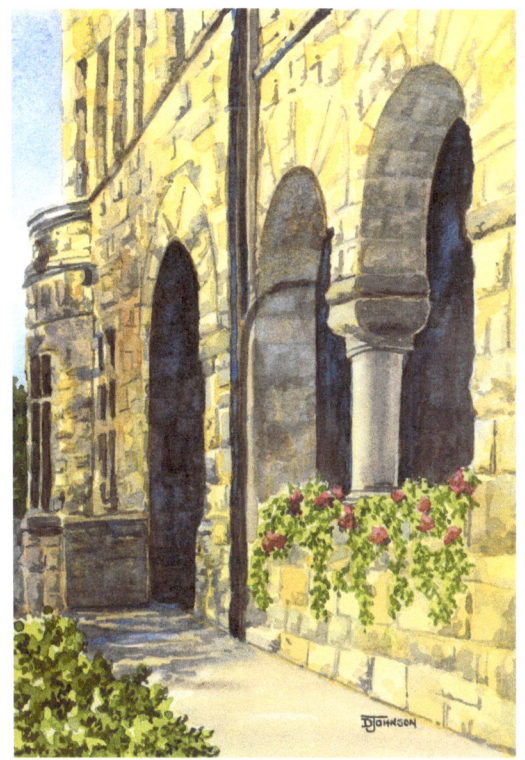

Arches and Geraniums

This cheery painting shows off the brush work for trees, plants and grass. Notice how simply the shadows on the lawn are painted. The message is conveyed without adding every blade of grass.

Be patient. These paintings took hours to complete! The time spent in preparation and practice made the actual painting process a lot of fun!

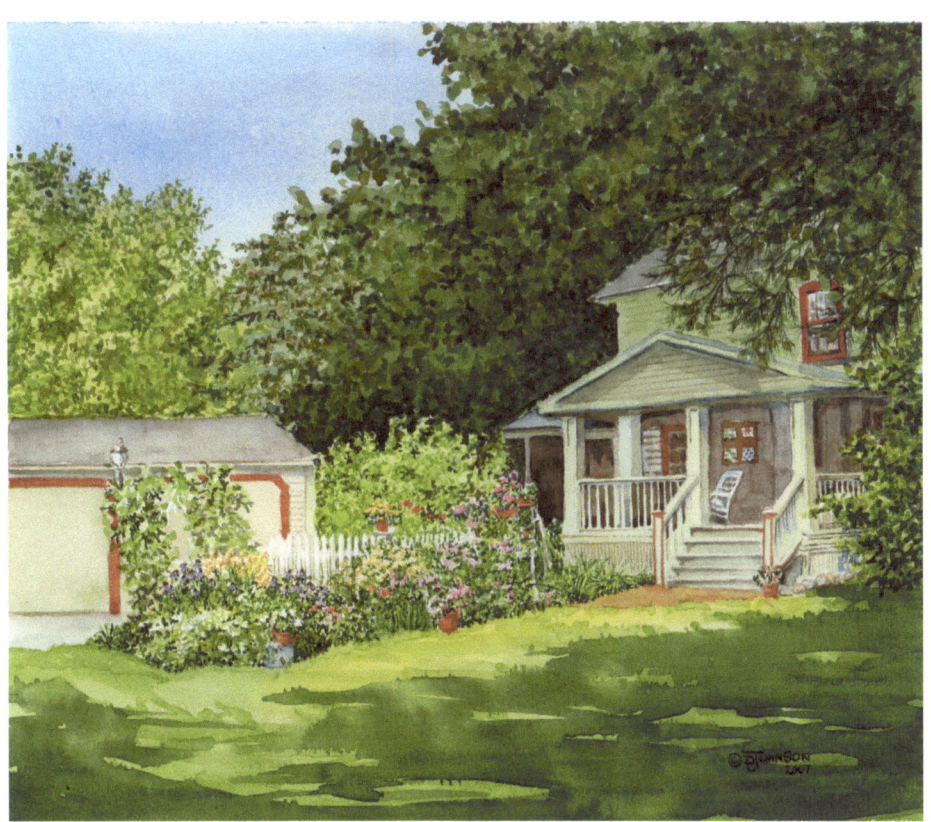

The Hepp House

Reference Photos

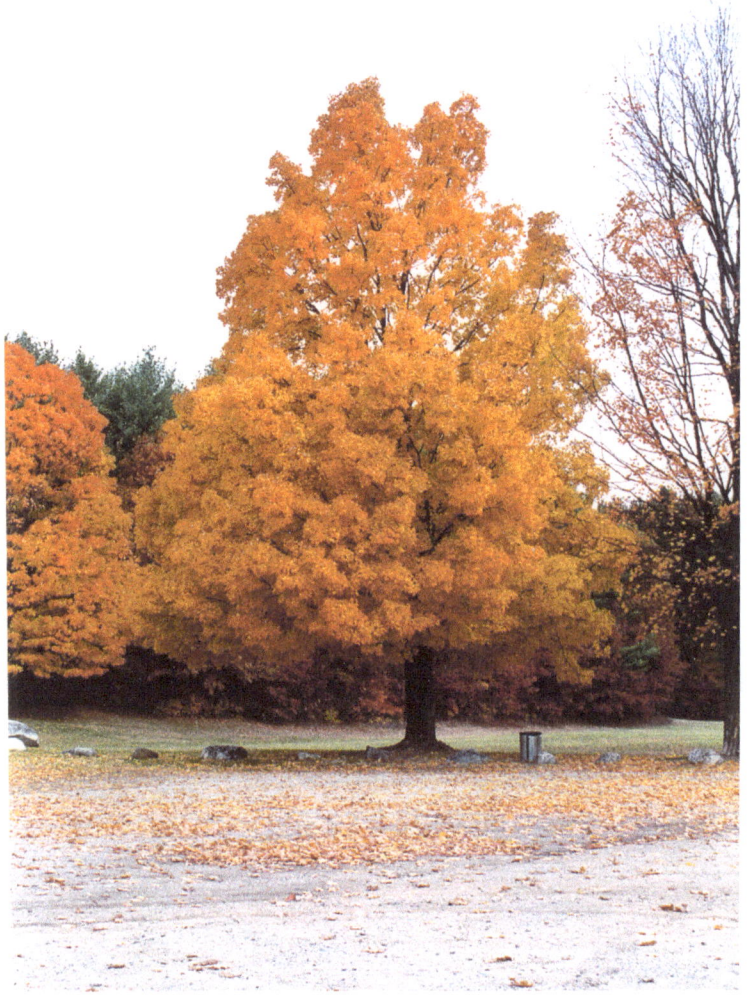

Removing the color from the reference photo helps me to see the values – the lights and darks – that give the two dimensional surface of the photo an illusion of space and shape.

Look at the value chart below and try to see where those values are represented in the grayscale photo reference.

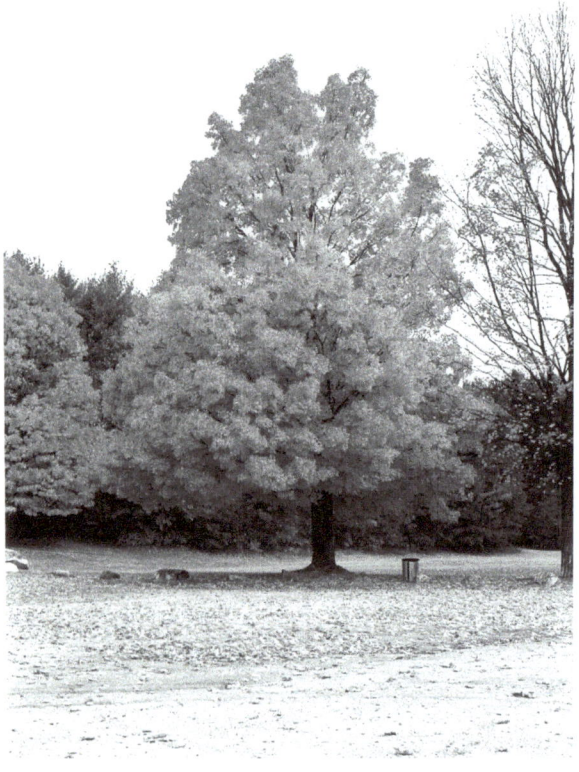

Photo reference used for sample painting project.

I hope you enjoyed this project. Please visit my website/blog and let me know your thoughts for future lessons!

www.debbiejohnsonartist.wordpress.com

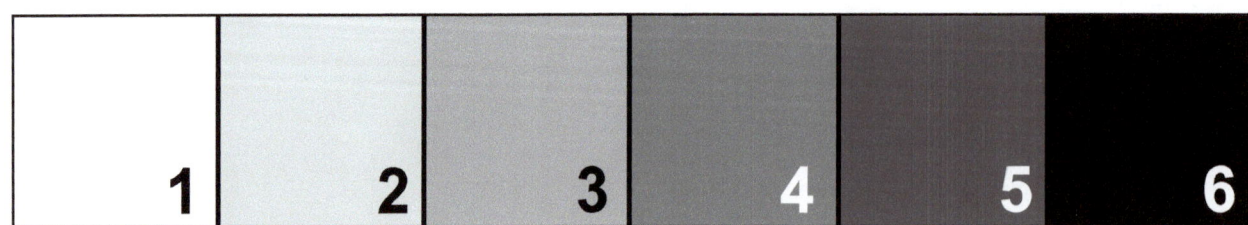

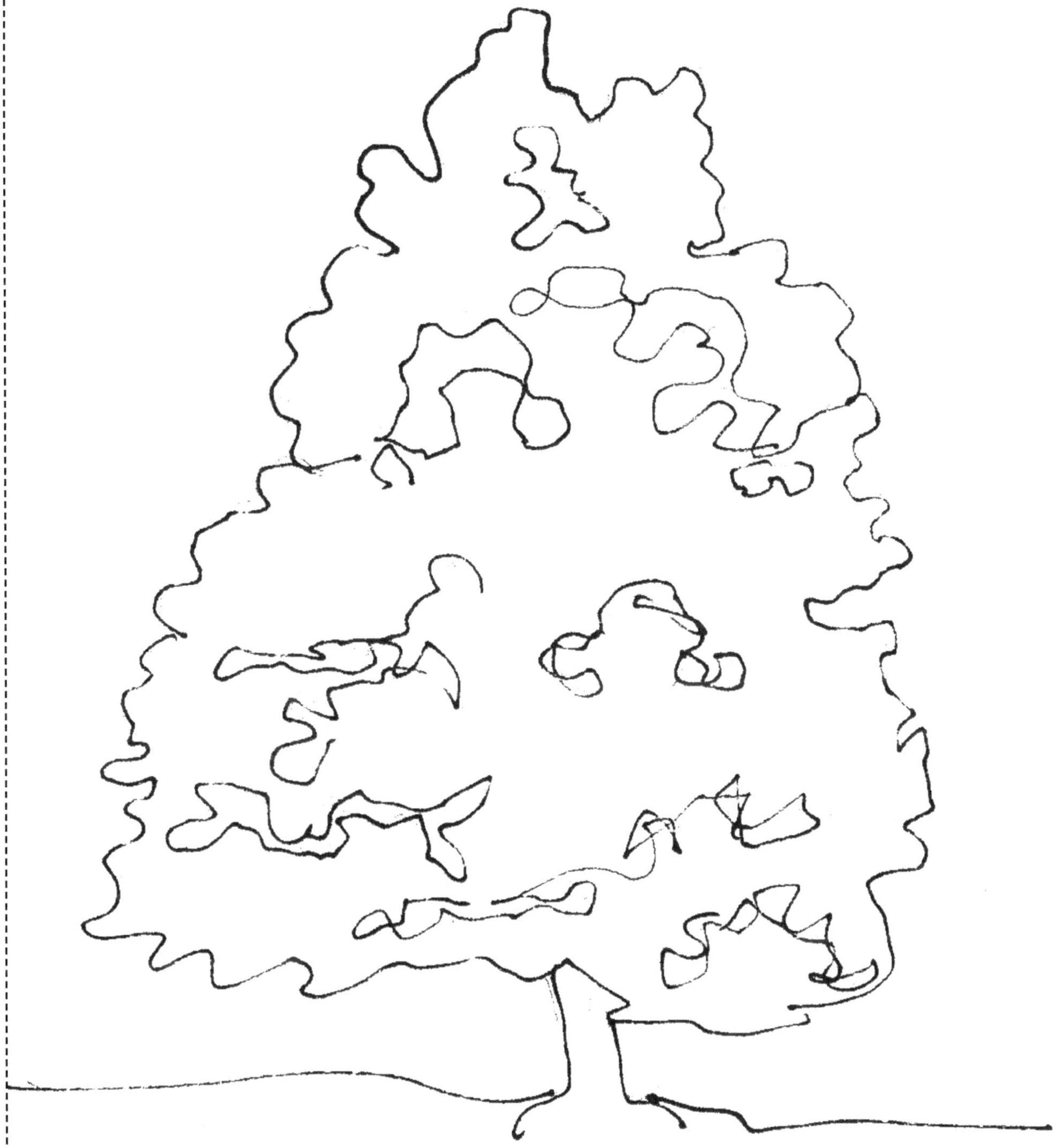

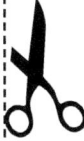

This drawing can be traced onto watercolor paper for practice.
This page may be copied or enlarged for your personal use only.

Suggested Watercolor Supplies

- 11" x 14" inch pad of Arches 140 lb. watercolor paper, or larger
- One-inch flat brush, natural hair, or natural hair/synthetic blend
- Number10 round brush, natural hair or natural hair/synthetic blend
- Number 6 round brush, natural hair or natural hair/synthetic blend
- Palette with large mixing wells and one-inch or wider paint wells. My favorite palette is CheapJoes Piggy Back.
- Winsor & Newton (professional grade/not student grade) pigments: Aureolin Yellow, New Gamboge, Winsor Red, Permanent Alizarin Crimson, Burnt Sienna, Perylene Maroon, VanDyke Brown, Raw Umber, Hookers Green, Cerulean Blue, French Ultramarine Blue, Indigo. Any other colors you may like to use. Other good brands are: Maimeriblu, Holbein, and Daler-Rowney. Look for transparent colors.
- White vinyl eraser
- Sketchbook, any kind
- Large water container (1 lb. deli tub works great)
- Paper towels
- Number 2 pencil
- Two-inch wide masking tape (not blue painter's tape)

Have fun experimenting with colors, brushes, and techniques. Every artist has his or her favorite tools and methods which is what makes each artist unique.

Great Online Art Supply Resources:
www.cheapjoes.com
jerrysartarama.com
www.dickblick.com
www.aswexpress.com
www.utrechtart.com
www.artsuppliesonline.com
Be sure to check with your local art supply store first.

Debbie Waldorf Johnson has more lessons on her website:
http://debbiejohnsonartist.wordpress.com/Lessons
You will find step-by-step lessons in blog format as well as links to videos of how to correctly develop watercolor washes.